THIS BOOK BELONGS TO:

_____

_____

HAND ME DOWN

♥

_____

To the bravest explorer I know: Jaali. Mommy loves you more than
words can say and you inspire me with every wolf howl you make.

To the children of the world: nature is yours to share.
For every bit you take and gain from it, give right back
to it with a thank you and a smile. Take care.

♥
ARJ

Written by Ashley Renee Jefferson. Illustrations by Kristiana Vellucci.
With consulting from Julia Moss.

ISBN: 979-8-9867049-2-0
LCCN: 2022918147

This book was printed in China in November 2022.

First edition
5 4 3 2 1

For questions regarding permissions, sales, or discounts,
email us at hello@littlefeminist.com.

ALL OF ME IS NATURE

EXPLORING MY FIVE SENSES OUTSIDE

by Ashley Renee Jefferson

little feminist press

All of me is nature
From my head down to my feet
So many ways to see it
Nature is part of me

What can you see in nature?

Bountiful trees, a dark hollow log
Or wings of a butterfly

Mountains or hills
Coral so still
Or light from a starry sky

All of me is nature,
From my head down to my feet,
So many ways to <u>feel</u> it,
Nature is part of me

What can you feel in nature?

The cold of snow
Velvety petals
Or spikes on sweet gum balls

The flow of water when I drink
Or rushing waterfalls

All of me is nature
From my head down to my feet
So many ways to <u>smell</u> it
Nature is part of me

What can you smell in nature?

The coniferous pine
The dirt and soil
Rosemary, sage or dill

Cedar wood
And the dampest of moss
Or plants on the window sill

All of me is nature
From my head down to my feet
So many ways to <u>taste</u> it
Nature is part of me

What can you taste in nature?

The seedy strawberry
A tart red cherry
Or arugula with all its spice

A pepper's crisp, a carrot's tip
Or the sweetness of a
watermelon slice

All of me is nature
From my head down to my feet
So many ways to <u>hear</u> it
Nature is part of me

What can you hear in nature?

Crunchy leaves from walking feet
Or giggles all around

An owl's hoot
A watering can
Acorns falling to the ground

All of me is nature
From my head down to my feet
So many ways to <u>be</u> it
Nature is part of me

How are you part of nature?

With every single move I make,
I am breathing air

With all the ways I play today,
I handle the earth with care

A NOTE FOR GROWNUPS

Not all people use the same senses (e.g., people who are deaf/blind, or who cannot smell/taste), and we all have different environments outside of our homes. No matter where we live, or how our bodies sense – the magic of nature is that it surrounds us all. Make sure to grab this book for your next outdoor adventure and use it to discuss caring for our environment.

ABOUT LITTLE FEMINIST

LittleFeminist.com is a children's book club subscription and publishing house. Our team curates the best diverse books, creates accompanying discussion questions and activities, and delivers to families around the world. We publish books to fill the gaps we find in children's literature.